MEASURE IT!

SPEED AND ACCELERATION

Barbara A. Somervill

Heinemann
LIBRARY

Chicago, Illinois

www.heinemannraintree.com
Visit our website to find out more information about Heinemann-Raintree books.

To order:
☎ Phone 888-454-2279
🖳 Visit www.heinemannraintree.com to browse our catalog and order online.

Edited by Megan Cotugno, Louise Galpine, and Abby Colich
Designed by Richard Parker
Original illustrations © Darren Lingard 2009
Picture research by Mica Brancic
Originated by Capstone Global Library, Ltd.
Printed and bound in China by CTPS

13 12 11 10
10 9 8 7 6 5 4 3 2

Library of Congress Cataloging-in-Publication Data

Somervill, Barbara A.
  Speed and acceleration / Barbara A. Somervill.
     p. cm. -- (Measure it!)
  Includes bibliographical references and index.
  ISBN 978-1-4329-3764-5 (hc) -- ISBN 978-1-4329-3770-6 (pb) 1. Speed--Measurement--Juvenile literature. 2. Acceleration (Mechanics)--Measurement--Juvenile literature. I. Title.
  QC137.52.S64 2010
  531'.112--dc22
                          2009035204

Acknowledgments

The author and publishers are grateful to the following for permission to reproduce copyright material:

Corbis pp. **6** (©John Bartholomew), **11** (©David Madison), **19** (©cultura), **21** (© UMA/PCN/PCN); Getty Images p. **20** (Dorling Kindersley/Gary Kevin); iStockphoto pp. **7** (©Grafissimo), **9** (©Kirill Putchenko), **13** (©James Boulette); Science Photo Library p. **16** (©U.S. Department of Defense); Shutterstock pp. **14** (© pjcross), **15** (© ceshot1), **22** (©Brendan Howard), **25** (©Daseaford), **28** (©Dennis Donohue).

Cover photo of a speed blur reproduced with permission from iStockphoto (©Peter Austin).

We would like to thank John Pucek for his invaluable help in the preparation of this book.

Every effort has been made to contact copyright holders of any material reproduced in this book. Any omissions will be rectified in subsequent printings if notice is given to the publisher.

All the Internet addresses (URLs) given in this book were valid at the time of going to press. However, due to the dynamic nature of the Internet, some addresses may have changed, or sites may have changed or ceased to exist since publication. While the author and Publishers regret any inconvenience this may cause readers, no responsibility for any such changes can be accepted by either the author or the Publishers.

Contents

Some words are printed in bold, **like this**. You can find out what they mean by looking in the glossary on page 30.

What Is Motion?

We are always in motion. Even when we sit perfectly still, our bodies remain in motion. Your chest moves in and out as you breathe, your heart beats, and blood moves through veins and arteries. Even if we do not count the normal motion in our bodies, we are still in motion. The Earth is always moving. Because of that, everything on the Earth is also always moving.

night

day

The Earth is always in motion, and all the people on the planet are moving, too.

Comparing motion

Motion can be slow, **moderate**, or fast. To decide if something is slow or fast, we compare rates of motion with other moving things. The Malaspina **glacier** in Alaska moves very slowly down a mountainside. The 3,880 square kilometer- (1,500 square mile-) glacier may move less than 100 meters (330 feet) every year. However, when the glacier melts, the icy water is freed to rush downhill much faster. A runner sprinting in a race seems fast, but that runner does not move as fast as a galloping racehorse. Cars and trains are faster than racehorses but slower than jet planes.

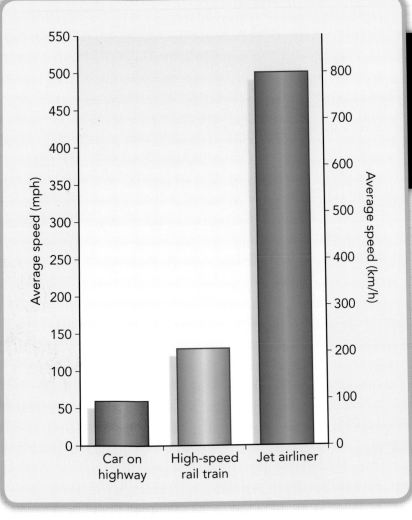

Estimating motion

We measure motion in many ways. Sometimes we **estimate** how fast something moves. We might say, "I can walk to school in about an hour." Other times we figure out an average **speed**. A man walks around a 10-kilometer (6-mile) track in 2 hours, so he walks at a rate of 5 kilometers (3 miles) per hour. We use exact measurements in timing races. Swimming, skiing, and running races are measured to the hundredth of a second.

Motion is the result of a **force** acting on a body. Simply put, force is a push or pull. The force can be natural, like the wind or waves. Leaves move from the force of wind. The force of ocean waves moves a boat toward the shore.

Gravity and friction

Gravity is another force that causes motion. Gravity is a universal force that acts between all objects. Anything that has **mass** also has gravitational pull. Mass is a property of the **matter** that makes up an object. For example, this book is made up of matter and has mass. Its mass comes from the paper, ink, and glue that make up the book. The force of gravity between two objects is always equal and opposite. However, if one of the objects has less mass, it will have a larger **acceleration** due to gravity than the object with the greater mass.

While some forces increase motion, other forces slow motion. **Friction** is the force that acts on the surface of an object as it moves over something else. Friction is resistance as a body moves or rolls over a surface. A car moves along a road. Friction works against the tires as they roll over the road.

Gravity caused these apples to fall from the tree to the ground.

Let's look at all the forces acting on a soccer ball on a grassy field. The gravitational force between the Earth and the ball pulls the ball toward the Earth. Wind blows and pushes against the ball. A person kicks the ball. The ball moves forward and skids along the grass. As the ball rolls over the grass, friction slows the ball down.

One force that acts on a soccer ball in a game is a human foot.

You Do the Math

The track coach wants to choose the fastest team for the 4 x 100-meter relay. Use the following chart to decide which four runners should be on the team. If each girl runs her fastest, what will be their combined times at the end of the race?

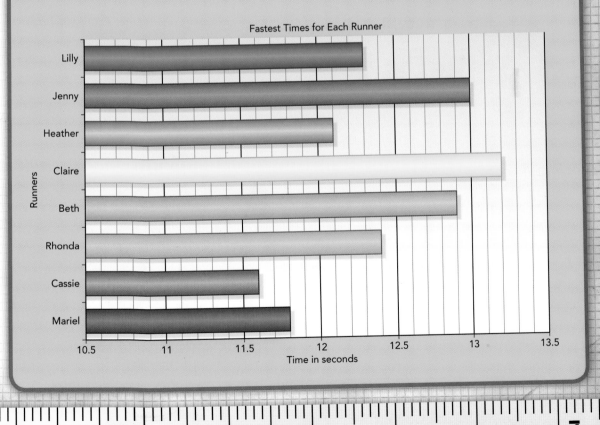

Fastest Times for Each Runner

What Is Speed?

One of the most common word problems in math goes something like this: A car travels 160 kilometers (100 miles) from Oakville to Elmdale. It takes 2 hours to make the trip. How fast was the car going? The answer is 80 kilometers (50 miles) per hour. That **speed** is an average speed, not a constant speed.

Speed measures how fast an object moves. Speeds over long distances are measured in kilometers per hour (km/h) or miles per hour (mph). Speeds over a short distance can be measured in meters or yards per minute or second, or feet per second.

The formula for determining speed is: rate equals distance divided by time, or r = d ÷ t. Knowing any two factors lets you figure out the third factor. You can work out distance by multiplying rate and time, or time by dividing distance by the rate.

You Do the Math

Two people, A and B, are driving in their cars. Read the speeds on both speedometers. Which driver is traveling at the faster speed? How much faster is that driver traveling?

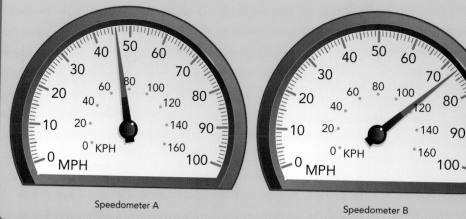

Speedometer A

Speedometer B

Velocity

With speed, the direction in which an object moves does not matter. When speed and direction are combined, they make **velocity**. Velocity is the rate of motion in a specific direction.

Natural and mechanical forces

Natural **forces** can produce speed. Moving air and water may cause tremendous damage. A tornado is a wind moving at great speed. Weather reports give two rates of speed for a tornado. One rate is how fast the tornado moves over land. The other rate is how fast air spins inside the tornado. Humans and animals are also natural forces that can produce speed. Snails move slowly, humans move at **moderate** speed, and cheetahs race at great speed.

When machines produce speed, they create mechanical forces. Gasoline, jet fuel, coal, steam, and electricity power engines to produce motion. Humans can power machines—scooters and bicycles—to move at speed.

The wind inside this dangerous tornado moved at speeds of 333 to 418 km/h (207 to 260 mph).

If you have to be at school at a certain time, you figure out when to leave home to get there on time. You work out the average speed for traveling to school. Air travel schedules and train schedules work the same way. They are set according to the speed needed to travel from one place to the next.

Record speeds

In motor sports, drivers and mechanics constantly work to make their vehicles move faster and faster. Some speed demons have produced record speeds. Those records change when a faster super car, boat, or jet is built.

Record Land, Air, and Water Speeds

Record	Vehicle	Speed in mph	Speed in km/h
Land speed by a car October 15, 1997	Thrust Supersonic Car	763 mph	1,228 km/h
Land speed by a motorcycle September 24, 2009	BUB Seven Streamliner	367.382 mph	580.8 km/h
Unmanned aircraft November 16, 2004	NASA X-43A	7,546 mph	12,144 km/h
Helicopter August 11, 1986	Westland Lynx 800	249.1 mph	401 km/h
Water speed October 8, 1978	Spirit of Australia	317.6 mph	511.1 km/h

The speed of a race car changes as the driver takes turns on the track, but race car speeds are given as the average speed per lap.

What Units Are Used When Measuring Speed?

A policeman sits in a car, pointing a radar gun at oncoming cars. A radar gun records **speed**. A car approaches going 52 mph in a 35 mph zone. This driver is getting a ticket!

We use several different units to measure speed. Common metric speed units include kilometers per hour (km/h) and meters per second (m/s). The most common imperial or U.S. customary units are miles per hour (mph) and feet per second (ft./s). The speed of ships at sea and planes in the air are measured in knots per hour. One knot per hour equals about 1.85 km/h (1.152 mph). Military jets and rockets travel at mach speed. Mach 1 equals the speed of sound at sea level, which is about 1,225 km/h (761 mph). Mach speed changes with **altitude**, air temperature, and humidity.

Imperial and Metric Conversions for Common Speed Measurements

Convert from...	...to	Multiply by...	Examples
mph	km/h	1.6	50 mph = 80 km/h
km/h	mph	0.62	100 km/h = 62 mph
m/s	ft./s	3.28	5 m/s = 16.4 ft./s
ft./s	m/s	0.31	10 ft./s = 3.1 m/s
knot	mph	1.15	10 knots = 11.5 mph
knot	km/h	1.852	10 knots = 18.52 km/h

A conversion chart makes it easy to switch from one measurement system to another.

Radar guns are used to record the speed of pitches in softball and baseball.

Speedometers

Radar measures the speeds of cars on roads. We also use radar to record the speed of baseball pitches and tennis serves. Another way to measure speed is with a speedometer. Speedometers can be used in all types of vehicles. The meter is attached to a wheel. As the wheel moves, the rate of spinning is converted into kilometers or miles per hour.

An anemometer measures how fast the wind is moving. As the cups spin, a gauge or meter records the speed at which they move.

Anemometers

Anemometers can save people's lives. They measure the speed of wind. Anemometers measure wind that is too strong for air or sea travel to be safe. They tell the wind speed of gales, hurricanes, and other major storms. Most anemometers look like cups on the end of a stick. The wind blows against the cups and makes the cups and stick spin. A meter beneath the stick reads the wind speed based on how fast the cups spin.

Stopwatches

Watches and stopwatches can help us measure rate of speed. Runners, skiers, and swimmers use stopwatches to measure their times over a course. They can compare their current times with earlier practices or races to see if they are moving with greater speed.

A coach uses a stopwatch to time how quickly an athlete covers a distance.

You Do the Math

Two trains travel between Toronto and Montreal. The train leaving Toronto travels at 64 mph. The Montreal train travels at 97 km/h. Which train is traveling faster?

How Fast Is Fast?

When the Concorde jet took off over Heathrow airport, its **speed** produced a sonic boom. Car alarms all around the airport went off. Windows rattled in people's homes, and a bang as loud as thunder broke the silence.

There are two speeds that are considered super fast. The first is the speed of sound. The second is the speed of light.

When jet pilots break the sound barrier, the sonic boom can be heard over a long distance.

Breaking the sound barrier happens when a jet travels 1,225 km/h (761 mph) at sea level. Sound waves are vibrations that travel through the air to produce sound. When a jet or other object travels faster than the speed of sound, people hear a sonic boom, which sounds like dynamite exploding.

Sound does not move in a line. It spreads out in a circle. Some jets can travel faster than sound moves. When the jet catches up to its own sound, there is a sound explosion. That explosion is called a sonic boom.

The first person to fly through the sound barrier was U.S. Air Force pilot Chuck Yeager in 1947 in a Bell X-1 jet. Today, most military jets travel fast enough to break the sound barrier.

In 1956 British engineers began working to design a supersonic passenger jet. The first Concorde made test flights in England and France in 1969. By the mid-1970s, the Concorde supersonic jet began flying a regular schedule between the United States and Europe. A Concorde flight from London to New York took just over three hours, less than half the time of traveling on a regular airliner. Supersonic travel was expensive and short-lived. More than two and a half million passengers flew on the Concorde before the flights ended in 2003.

Speed of light

If sound travels fast, light travels even faster. The speed of light is measured as light travels through a **vacuum**, with no air, dust particles, or any other **matter** in the way. It takes about eight minutes for light to travel from the sun to the Earth. Our galaxy is so big that traveling at the speed of light from one end to the other would take about 100,000 years.

So just what kind of speed are we talking about? In a vacuum, light moves at 299,792,458 m/s. In the 1900s, Albert Einstein came up with the idea that no object could ever move faster than the speed of light. Some physicists disagree. They have been doing research to break the speed of light limit. In 2000 experiments showed that energy pulses (bursts of pure energy) could travel faster than light.

How fast is fast? If today's scientists can be believed, there may be no limit to speed. What will the measure of this new speed be? We'll have to wait and see.

What Is Acceleration?

A car moves onto a highway. Coming off a side road, the car is only going 65 km/h (40 mph). The driver presses down on the accelerator and the car quickly increases **speed**. In just a few seconds, the car increases speed to 95 km/h (60 mph). The car smoothly enters the highway and merges with traffic.

Most people think that **acceleration** means increasing speed. That is not true. Acceleration can be either an increase or a decrease in speed. Acceleration is actually a change in the speed. That change is measured by the second. Slowing down is acceleration in an opposite direction.

Both speeding up and slowing down are forms of acceleration. A driver needs to know how quickly a car speeds up to move into heavy traffic. That same driver needs to know how fast brakes can slow the car to avoid an accident. An airport builds a new runway. The runway must be long enough for a jet to increase speed for takeoff or to slow down when landing.

Brakes change acceleration. They use **friction** to produce acceleration in the opposite direction.

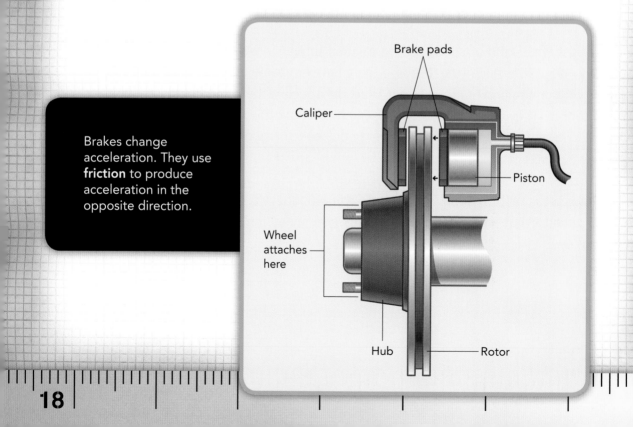

Brake pads

Caliper

Piston

Wheel attaches here

Hub

Rotor

Positive and negative acceleration

Acceleration happens when a **force** acts on an object. The larger the **mass** of the object, the greater amount of force needed to accelerate the object. Let's look at force and both positive and negative acceleration.

A car and a bicycle are on a flat surface. A ten-year-old boy pushes each one. He has no success moving the car. He cannot exert enough force to move the car. He easily moves the bicycle forward. This is called positive acceleration. The bicycle has less mass, so less force is needed to accelerate it.

Now let's think about negative acceleration. Grass on a hill creates **friction**, which acts as a negative force to slow the speed of objects moving over it. A basketball and a golf ball are placed on top of the hill. Each is pushed with equal force. Which one will roll farther? The answer is the basketball. Why? The frictional forces acting on the golf ball slow it down.

This man can produce enough force to push a bicycle, but not a car.

Forcemeters

We use **forcemeters** to measure the amount of force acting on an object. The units used when measuring force are **Newtons**, a unit named for Sir Isaac Newton (see box). The rate of force equals the mass of an object times the acceleration of the object, or f = m x a.

Sir Isaac Newton
Some people say that Sir Isaac Newton (1642–1727) developed the theory of **gravity** when an apple fell on his head. This is probably not true, but Newton was a brilliant mathematician and scientist in England. He owned an orchard, and, watching ripe apples fall to the ground, realized that there was a force that made the apple drop. He figured that the same force kept the moon in space and planets orbiting around the sun. Newton also figured out that gravity causes the tides. And all of this was done without a calculator!

Forcemeters measure force in Newtons, a unit of measure named for Sir Isaac Newton.

You Do the Math

The following is a chart of acceleration rates for a top level sprinter in a 100-meter race. Use the chart below to answer the questions.

Time in seconds	Speed in m/s	Average acceleration in m/s^2
1	5.35	5.35
2	7.80	2.45
3	9.5	1.7
4	10	0.50
5	10.38	0.38
6	10.50	0.12
7	10.50	0
8	10.30	-0.20
9	9.90	-0.40
10	9.30	-0.60
11	8.25	-1.05

1. At what point is there no acceleration?
2. At what point in the race has the runner reached maximum speed?
3. At what time in the race is the acceleration rate highest?
4. When the runner crosses the finish line, is she still accelerating?

What Units Are Used When Measuring Acceleration?

An engineer is designing an engine for a new jet plane. The engine must create enough **force** to accelerate the jet for takeoff. If the engine does not produce the needed force, the jet will crash at the end of the runway. The engineer needs to know the **mass** of the jet when it is full. Every passenger, piece of luggage, cargo crate, fuel, and even cans of soda add mass.

The acceleration of a jet on takeoff must be great enough to lift the plane off the ground.

The engineer also needs to think about the forces acting on the jet that cause negative **acceleration** or a decrease in **speed**. These forces include wind, air, **friction**, and **gravity**. Getting a jet off the ground gives an engineer a lot to think about.

Acceleration is usually recorded on charts or graphs that show increase or decrease in speed over time. Units used when measuring acceleration are meters per second squared (m/s^2) or feet per second squared ($ft./s^2$). When converting from metric to imperial or U.S. customary measurement, 1 m/s^2 equals 3.28 $ft./s^2$. Converting the other way, 1 $ft./s^2$ equals 0.304 m/s^2. Acceleration measures for sports and most vehicles are usually measured in m/s^2.

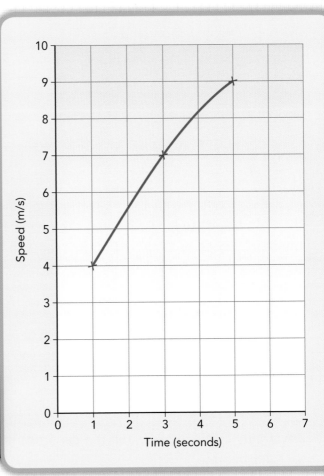

To record acceleration, use a chart or a graph.

Engineers, sports coaches, and athletes work with acceleration all the time. They need to know how much effort is needed to make an object move faster. They also need to know how to slow down a moving object. Figuring out the acceleration of a vehicle requires some advanced mathematics. Although the formula looks complicated, it is not difficult.

Calculating acceleration

Let's use an example to work through the math. A high-speed train travels from Tokyo to Kyoto in Japan. The train quickly reaches a traveling speed of 31 m/s, which is the final maximum speed. It took 20 seconds to reach its fastest speed from a standing point. How can we find the rate of acceleration of the train? Use this formula:

acceleration = (final velocity − beginning velocity) ÷ time, or

$a = (vf - vi) \div t$

$a = (31 \text{ m/s} - 0 \text{ m/s}) \div 20 \text{ s}$

acceleration of the train = 1.55 m/s^2

At the start of the trip, the train is not moving at all. The engines turn, and the train begins to move. Finding the acceleration means finding how quickly the train's **velocity** increased until it reached its top speed. Since it only took 20 seconds to reach a speed of 31 m/s, the train's acceleration was 1.55 m/s².

We can also use the same formula to figure out negative acceleration. If you are going to figure out how to go faster, you also need to figure out how to stop. Engineers who design cars need to figure this for every car they make.

Let's look at the braking power of a car. A car travels at about 30 m/s. The driver puts on the brakes, and the car stops in 6 seconds. Let's figure out the acceleration rate.

acceleration = final velocity − beginning velocity ÷ time, or

$a = vf - vi \div t$

$a = 0 \text{ m/s} - 30 \text{ m/s} \div 6 \text{ s}$

acceleration of the car = $- 5 \text{ m/s}^2$

Measuring negative acceleration

Measuring negative acceleration (slowing down) works the same way as measuring positive acceleration. A dog runs into the road, and the driver puts on the brakes to stop. The **velocity** the car is going once it stops is 0 m/s. When the driver put on the brakes, the car was moving at 30 m/s. Working out negative acceleration means working with negative numbers. You are subtracting a rate of speed from 0. In this case, you subtract 30 from 0 to get -30. Do the math the same way you do with positive numbers. Just remember to include the minus sign to show the acceleration is negative.

Calculating acceleration force

We can also figure out the force needed to accelerate a vehicle if we know the mass and the rate of acceleration. Force, measured in **Newtons** (N), equals the mass (in kg) multiplied by the acceleration (in m/s^2). The mass of a bicycle is 8 kg. The bicycle accelerates at 5 m/s^2. The force needed to move the bicycle is 8 kg x 5 m/s^2, or 40 N.

You Do the Math

The mass of a car is 900 kg. It accelerates at 12 m/s^2. What is the force exerted to move the car at this rate?

Which Horse Goes the Fastest?

A carousel goes around and around. The lights dazzle our eyes. The music is fast. Your horse is the fastest...or is it? Our carousel has four rows of horses, and each row makes a circle as it moves. All the horses, regardless of which row they are in, complete the circle in the same amount of time.

The horses traveling along the outside of a carousel move faster to make one circle of the carousel in the same time as horses on the inner rows.

Do all the horses on a carousel really travel at the same **speed**? No, they do not. The circle made by a horse on the inside row has a **radius** of 5 meters (m). The circle made by a horse on the outside row has a radius of 10 m. On this carousel, the distance around the inside circle is 31 m. The distance around the outside circle is 62 m. Going all the way around the outside circle is twice as far as the inside circle.

The distance around the outside circle is twice as long as the distance around the inside circle.

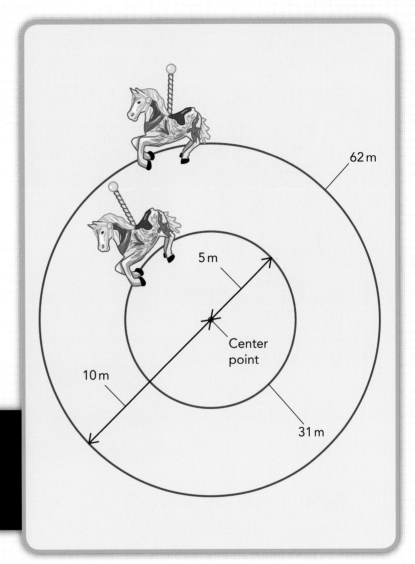

62 m

5 m

Center point

10 m

31 m

Suppose it takes 2 minutes (min.) for our carousel to make one rotation. We have everything we need to figure out speed. The speed of any object equals the distance it travels divided by the time. The inside horse travels 31 meters in 2 min., so its speed is 15.5 m/min. The outside horse travels 62 m in 2 min., so its speed is 31 m/min. Next time you ride on a carousel, choose an outside horse if you want a faster ride!

The horse running farthest from the fence on this oval track will need to run faster to win the race.

Racing around a track

How does a carousel relate to real life? Suppose you are running a race. A racetrack is usually an oval. If you run along the inside of the track, you will travel a shorter distance than if you run along the outside. If you get stuck running on the outside of your fellow runners, you will need to run much faster than they do to win. If you position yourself along the inside, you just need to worry about your speed and **acceleration**. This is also true of horse races, which is why jockeys work hard to get a spot along the inside rail. They don't want to make their horse run farther than other horses to win!

Answers to You Do the Math

What Is Motion? (page 7)

The coach should choose Cassie, Emily, Heather, and Lilly. If each runs her fastest, the finishing time will be 11.6 s + 11.8 s + 12.1 s + 12.3 s = 47.8 s.

What Is Speed? (page 8)

Driver B is traveling faster. Subtract: 73 mph – 46 mph = 27 mph. B is going 27 mph faster than A.

What Units Are Used When Measuring Speed? (page 15)

Convert the speed of the Toronto train to km/h: 64 mph x 1.6 = 102.4 km/h. The Toronto train is traveling 5.4 km/h faster than the Montreal train.

What Is Acceleration? (page 21)

1. There is no acceleration at the 7-second mark.
2. The runner reaches maximum speed at 6 seconds.
3. Acceleration rate is highest in the first second.
4. Yes, the runner's speed is changing. Acceleration is going in the opposite direction at the end of the race.

What Units Are Used When Measuring Acceleration? (page 25)

Force = mass x acceleration
$F = 900 \text{ kg} \times 12 \text{ m/s}^2 = 10,800 \text{ N}$

Glossary

acceleration rate of change of velocity with respect to time

altitude height above sea level

anemometer tool used to measure wind speed

estimate make an approximate guess

force a push or pull

forcemeter machine for measuring the force exerted on an object

friction surface resistance against a moving object

glacier extremely large ice mass

gravity force of attraction that pulls two objects together

mass measure of how much matter or "stuff" an object contains

matter anything that has mass and occupies space

moderate of medium quantity or extent

Newton basic unit of force

radius distance from the center of a circle to the outside of the circle

speed rate of change of distance of an object with respect to time

vacuum empty space

velocity rate of movement in a direction of an object with respect to time

Find Out More

Books

Lepora, Nathan. *High Speed Thrills: Acceleration and Velocity*. Pleasantville, N.Y.: Gareth Stevens, 2008.

Schrier, Alison Valentine. *What If We Measured Speed as Feet Per Hour?* Logan, Iowa: Perfection Learning, 2006.

Schuh, Mari C. *Full Speed Ahead: The Science of Going Fast*. Danbury, Conn.: Children's Press, 2008.

Sullivan, Navin. *Measure Up! Speed*. Tarrytown, N.Y.: Benchmark Books, 2006.

Woodford, Chris. *Speed (How Do We Measure?)*. Farmington Hills, Mich.: Blackbirch Press, 2005.

Websites

BrainPOP
www.brainpop.com/science/motionsandforces/acceleration/
Watch a video about acceleration at this website.

PBS Measuring Speed
http://pbskids.org/zoom/activities/sci/measuringboatspeed.html
Use this website to figure out the speed of a moving object.

Science for Kids: Acceleration
www.historyforkids.org/scienceforkids/physics/movement/acceleration.htm
Visit this website to learn more about acceleration.

Index